Newcastl
of the
World

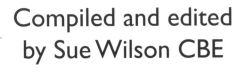

Compiled and edited
by Sue Wilson CBE

Foreword by
David Faulkner OBE

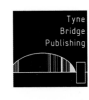

Tyne
Bridge
Publishing

Published by
Tyne Bridge Publishing 2018
City Library
Newcastle Upon Tyne
tynebridgepublishing.org.uk

Layout: David Hepworth

Foreword

The concept of 'twin towns', 'partner towns' or 'sister cities' ('ville Jumelée' in French or 'Comune gemellato' in Italian) has been understood for a long time. We are a group of towns and cities that value and see benefit through international connections, but we happen to have the same name! What better reason for choosing your friends to work with in other parts of the world?

There are over one hundred 'Newcastles all across the world that we know of – and we learn about more of them each year as we explore languages that are currently less familiar to us. We are keen to build contacts and find out more about their communities and way of life.

Most 'Newcastles' are not part of the Newcastles of the World alliance or network in any formalised way, but we are more than willing to develop and maintain some connection with them though our work, should they be wish it.

Newcastle upon Tyne - where I was a councillor and, for a while, Leader of the City Council - was not a founding member of our alliance. However, some of the early impetus behind the idea - of sharing knowledge about what we have in common and what we can learn from each other - came from this city. And a few years ago it was our privilege to have been asked by our sister and brother 'Newcastles' to provide a secretariat, to facilitate and promote the work that we do together. We have a group of local people here who assist in this task and who, between them, have wide experience of civic and community life and of international connections. Working with their counterparts in other 'Newcastles', they value and champion the principle of cooperation across national boundaries, to advance wider understanding and the common good.

David Faulkner, Coordinator, Newcastles of the World

Nest page, clockwise from top left: 1) Traditional dancing at Nové Zámky, 2) Young people from Neuchâtel join in celebrations in Shinshiro. 3) Newcastle, South Africa. 4) Castle festivities in Neuburg. 5) Medieval re-enactments at Newcastle upon Tyne. 6) Tominaga Shrine festival, Shinshiro.

A colourful celebration at the Neuchâtel Fête des vendanges.

Introduction

There are many places in the world named Newcastle. At one time they may have had castles. Some still do. Not all of them are English-speaking. There were new castles in many different countries resulting in names such as Shinshiro, Neuchâtel, Neuburg, and Nové Hrady. And some Newcastles were named after other Newcastles or individuals bearing the name Newcastle. Not all are cities, some are towns or even villages. One is an army settlement. One is a star. They all shine brightly in their own way.

In 1998 a network of Newcastles was formed when the mayor of Shinshiro in Japan invited a number of cities to Japan to attend the first summit of Newcastles. Eight attended and a conference has been held every two years since then in Newcastles around the world with the network gathering momentum and members along the way and spawning a number of youth and cultural projects.

At the same time as the gathering in Shinshiro I chaired a project in Newcastle upon Tyne to contact the Newcastles in the English-speaking world and capture a flavour of their cultural make-up in a publication. This was compiled by John Nicolaou and published in 2000. It featured twenty-five Newcastles in the UK, Ireland, USA, Canada, Australia, South Africa and the Caribbean.

Over time the two projects came together with the conference in the twentieth year of the network being held in Shinshiro in 2018 where it all began. Since I began attending the Newcastle of the World conferences in 2010 there have been many requests for another book to include more Newcastles and so, finally, here is that book. I am indebted to so many of our friends in Newcastles around the world who have contributed material and photographs to make this book possible. There are far too many to mention but I would particularly like to mention David Faulkner and Zelie Guerlin who have supplied much of the additional material needed from the network secretariat based in Newcastle upon Tyne. David has worked tirelessly to ensure that I could include photographs of the many Newcastles we are in touch with so far. There are over one hundred mentioned in this book but I have no doubt that there are many more to be discovered.

The Newcastles network has enabled a sharing of ideas, cultural exchanges for young people, tourism initiatives, celebrations of heritage, education support for underprivileged children and many joint cultural projects. Above all it is a friendship network bringing people and nations together to converse and celebrate diversity.

This publication is a celebration of the Newcastles of the World, all that has been achieved over the last twenty years and a glimpse of what the future might hold.

Sue Wilson CBE

The Castles

Not all of the Newcastles had a castle as some were named after other Newcastles and some castles are long gone, but a surprising number endure as reminders of a time when warfare was a more straightforward show of force.

Many of the 'new castles' date back to Norman times, that being the great age of European stone castle construction. Often they are on the site of a previous Roman fortification, the Romans having found the most strategic site for defence and control of the surrounding area.

In Newcastle upon Tyne, England, only the castle keep, the main fortified tower, and its fortified gatehouse, the Black Gate, remain. In Roman times the site was a defensive stronghold with a fort and settlement called Pons Aelius overseeing a bridge over the river Tyne. In 1080 a wooden castle was built there by the eldest son of William the Conquerer returning south from a Scottish campaign. The present stone keep was built between 1172 and 1177 by Henry II and still contains some Roman stone.

Above: Newcastle upon Tyne's Norman castle keep.
Right: Nyborg Castle festival.

2

The Château de Neuchâtel, Switzerland, was a castle begun in the 12th century, but, possibly with its origins in an earlier Novum Castellum first mentioned in 1011. It is an imposing building in the old town next to the parish church.

In Neuburg an der Donau, Germany, the castle dates back to medieval times with Neuburg as a name first appearing in 1214 in parish records. Its current form as a stately palace owes its style to the first duke of the Palatinate-Neuburg Principality, who added high Renaissance gables and a beautiful courtyard surrounded by arcades in the 16th century. Later, Duke Phillip Wilhelm would add a Baroque Eastern wing and two round towers.

Neuburg Castle Festival.

Nyborg Castle, Denmark, was built around 1170 and is one of the oldest preserved royal palaces in Denmark. The kingdom's first constitution was signed here in 1282 and the foundations of the Danish parliamentary system laid here. It remained a royal power base until the mid 16th century. Nyborg Castle is currently being restored to its original size and shape and made accessible to the public.

New Castle, Nové Hrady.

The Czech town of Nové Hrady has two castles. The old one is a Gothic pass-through castle with two gateways situated on a fifty-metre high promontory and surrounded by a fourteen-metre deep moat. It came into the ownership of the Rozmberk family in 1358 and when their line died out in the 17th century it passed to the Count of Buquoy. The new castle was built in the early 19th century by the Buquoy family as a more fitting chateau residence and now houses the Institute of Physical Biology of the University of South Bohemia.

Old Castle, Nové Hrady.

Latvia's Jaunpils Castle was built in 1301 as a fortress for the Livonian Order and has remained mainly intact since then. Medieval-style feasts are now held in the banqueting hall under a vaulted ceiling.

Jaunpils Castle in Winter.

In Akhaltsikhe, Georgia the splendid medieval Rabati Castle complex covers seven hectares. The castle was originally surrounded by three lines of walls with gates and watchtowers and connected to the suburbs of the town by tunnels. A court, a mint, an arsenal, guest houses and bath house were contained within the complex. A previous castle was destroyed by wars in the 9th century. Bashquen II Jaqeli rebuilt the castle in the 12th century and named it Akhaltsikhe or New Castle.

Nové Zámky, Slovakia, became the centre of anti-Turk defence in Western Slovakia in the 16th century. The first castle was a wooden fortification built on the left bank of the Nitra River on land belonging to the archbishop of Ostrihom, Pavol Varday. The second, a Renaissance fortress was built on the river in 1573-1580 and designed by Italian architects, Ottavio and Giulio Baldigar. It had a hexagonal floor plan and a wide moat and was considered one of the best fortresses of the Hapsburg monarchy. It was eventually captured by the Ottoman army in 1663 and held for twenty-two years before being liberated. Charles III ordered its demolition in 1724.

Newcastle under Lyme, England, had a new castle built in the 12th century to replace an earlier one further north in the town, but by the 16th century the castle had vanished

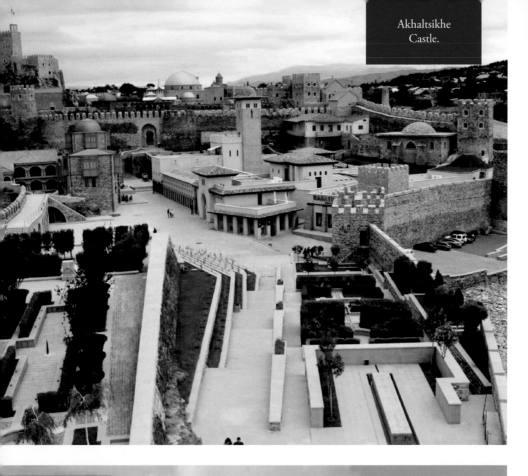

Akhaltsikhe Castle.

Neuburg an der Donau Castle.

Nové Zámky's hexagonal floor plan.

apart from 'one great Toure.' Today even the tower has gone leaving only a mound and some stonework.

The castle in Shinshiro, Japan, is long gone but was constructed in 1576 after the battle of Nagashi-shitaragahara by a victorious Nobumasa Okudaira. The site now houses an elementary school.

Sadly, many castles have been lost over the centuries to wars, fashion and development but records and legends keep their memories alive.

Dance of the Knights Tournament at Nyborg Castle.

Newcastle upon Tyne, United Kingdom
newcastle.gov.uk

Newcastle upon Tyne is a city of 300,000 people in North East England, not far from the border with Scotland. Its rich history dates to AD122 when Roman Emperor Hadrian built a bridge over the River Tyne and a fort on the overlooking hill for protection. The World Heritage site of 'Hadrian's Wall' was the northern frontier of the Roman Empire, stretching 120 km from east of Newcastle to the west coast.

In medieval times, the settlement became 'Monkchester', then 'Newcastle' with a new wooden castle in 1080, replaced by the present stone castle in 1172.

Newcastle's prosperity was built on wool, glass, pottery and coal - mined locally and shipped to the Baltic, Flanders and London. The Tyne soon became one of the world's great shipbuilding rivers - for over one hundred years.

It was also the home of the railways - the world's first locomotive factory – and the electric light bulb was first demonstrated here, forerunner to a world-leading power industry. These great engineering innovations, together with munitions and brewing (Newcastle Brown Ale) were at the industrial revolution's heart, before the industries began to decline.

Today, Newcastle is known for its theatres, museums and galleries; the annual Town Moor funfair (Europe's largest), its magnificent bridges across the river, Newcastle United football club and other sporting attractions like the Great North Run, the world's biggest half marathon.

The Tyne Bridge and the Newcastle and Gateshead Quayside along the River Tyne.

The city is easily reached via Newcastle International Airport, the Port of Tyne or frequent rail links to London and Edinburgh; it is simple to get around the city too using the Metro (underground) and the centre is easily navigated on foot whether to enjoy the 1830s neoclassical architectural beauty of 'Grainger Town', or the spectacular Quayside, to see one of England's 'Chinatowns', or the medieval city walls and castle or Blackfriars monastery.

Locals (known as 'Geordies') are friendly folk who enjoy Newcastle's exciting nightlife, but also its many restaurants, late night-shopping and year-round festivals and events.

Across the Tyne are three high-profile contemporary attractions - BALTIC Centre for Contemporary Art, The Sage Gateshead international music centre and the famous 'Angel of the North' sculpture. Also near is the stunning North East coast (or go further up to 'Holy Island'); and magnificent attractions like Alnwick Castle – a location for the first two Harry Potter films.

Newcastle is a vibrant retail and commercial centre, with two distinguished universities (Newcastle and Northumbria). Today's economy is based on professional services; offshore/marine and renewables; medical sciences and sustainability; and a strong digital and creative cluster.

Whilst the Newcastle area was home to great inventors and industrialists, it's more popularly known for entertainers such as Sting and Rowan Atkinson (Mr Bean), footballer Alan Shearer – and for Earl Grey, Prime Minister of England, but better known for the tea that bears his name.

Newcastle values its links with its many twin cities, including Atlanta, Bergen, Nancy and Gelsenkirchen. 'International Newcastle' is the city's networking agency, whilst tourism, inward investment and major festivals are promoted by NewcastleGateshead Initiative.

Grey's monument and the 'Best Street in Britain' - Grey Street.

A view of Newcastle upon Tyne (UK) in Elizabethan times. The castle in a prominent and defensible location. Painted by John Storey.

Shinshiro, Japan
city.shinshiro.lg.jp.e.ji.hp.transer.com

Located almost in the centre of Japan, Shinshiro is one and a half hours by train and Shinkansen (express train) to Tokyo to the north. Nagoya International airport is an hour and a half by car. In 2016, the interchange of a new Tomei expressway was established in Shinshiro improving connections to the major cities.

Shinshiro city has a population of 47,415 people (December 2017).

Shinshiro has a special place in Japanese history and is famous for the battle of Nagashino-shitaragahara. It was here that the allied forces of Oda and Tokugawa, who would later found the Tokugawa shogunate that ruled for nearly three centuries, crushed the forces of Takeda in the decisive battle in 1575.

The city has a strong connection to Ieyasu Tokugawa who is famous as the founder of the Edo period in Japanese history. Ieyasu's mother went to the Mt. Horaiji temple in Shinshiro to pray for the birth of child. Her prayers were answered and Ieyasu was born.

The new castle, Shinshiro, was built in 1576 by Nobumasa Okudaira who was decorated in the battle of Nagashino-shitaragahara. He married the eldest daughter of Ieyasu Tokugawa, Sen-hime, when she was seventeen years old. The castle is no longer standing and Shinshiro elementary school is built on the site.

There is no university in Shinshiro, but there is a nursing vocational school.

The economy of Shinshiro is a mixture of agriculture and industry. In addition to vegetables, rice and fruits it is a significant producer of tea. There is a strong indusrial base with factories and research institutes of world-renowned enterprises such as Yokohama Rubber, Mitsubishi Electric and Tonbow Stationery.

The city is full of tourist attractions, such as historical sites of the warring period, comfortable hot springs, festivals and local foods.

The hot spring village consists of nine Japanese style hotels along the river.

The hot water is believed to be therapeutic for many diseases and people enjoy relaxing in the waters observing the green forest and listening to the sound of streams.

Shinshiro has many sports events such as the Tour de Shinshiro which is a bicycle race, trail running which is a cross-country sport, running through natural forests and mountains and the Shinshiro Rally which is a motor sport.

Shinshiro is a sister city of Neuchâtel, Switzerland and student exchanges have taken place with Japanese high school students from Shinshiro, aged fifteen to seventeen, visiting Neuchatel and lodging with volunteer families, studying languages and enjoying discoveriing the region. The first Youth Conference of the Newcastles network took place in Shinshiro in 2017.

Top:
Tai Chi in a park full
of cherry blossoms.
Middle:
Horaisam Toshogu
Shrine dedicated to
the spirit of
Tokugausa Ieyasu.
Right:
A re-enactment of the
Battle of Shinshiro.

Neuchâtel, Switzerland
neuchatelville.ch

The first mention of 'Novum Castellum' (New Castle in Latin) in an official document dates from 1011. In ten centuries of a turbulent history, Neuchâtel was the property of French counts, the Orléans-Longueville, before passing into the hands of the King of Prussia. In the 19th century that Neuchâtel became a canton member of the Swiss Confederation, a canton to which the city gave its name.

Neuchâtel is located in the northwest of Switzerland, in the French speaking part of the country, near a large lake which also bears the name of the city. Leaning on the mountain, between vineyards and forests, Neuchâtel has its feet in the water. This privileged location allows its inhabitants to enjoy a still unspoilt nature in the heart of the city. It is pleasant to walk on the banks and have a good meal at the water's edge. The red and white wines of our hillsides make a charming accompaniment to the fish specialties of the lake or the local cheeses.

A city of 34,000 inhabitants, Neuchâtel applies its motto 'Lifestyle and Innovation' by combining the well-being of its population with a connected edge on technological developments. Neuchâtel offers a rich artistic, cultural and sporting life with a high-quality infrastructure: a theatre, five museums, a swimming pool, a skating rink and various sports grounds.

The French writer Alexandre Dumas saw Neuchâtel as 'a gem cut in butter', referring to the famous yellow stone used to build most buildings in the city. Today its historical heritage, is maintained with care. It is in this pleasant cocoon that a dynamic local life develops characterised by a wide offer in shops, a strong community and cultural events of international scope.

City of the famous chocolatier Philippe Suchard, Neuchâtel organises a festival every autumn dedicated to 'Chocolatissimo'. Summer is punctuated by the Neuchâtel International Fantastic Film Festival and the music of Festi'Neuch which hosts groups from around the world. For more than a century, the Wine Harvest Festival has been paying tribute to the Neuchâtel vineyards, attracting hundreds of thousands of visitors for three days in September.

As a training town, Neuchâtel is home to a university and several research institutes specializing in micro and nanotechnologies and especially in solar energy which makes Neuchâtel a world leader in photovoltaic research. Micro technology is not new in Neuchâtel and the Museum of Art and History hosts the famous Jaquet-Droz automata, three androids designed in the 18th century and the real ancestors of our computers, which are demonstrated every month.

Valuing the environment and sustainable development, the city leads an exemplary energy policy that earned it the 2006 'European Energy Award Gold' label.

Neuchâtel is an open and internationally active city. It participates in several Council of Europe projects, particularly in the area of integration. It has been a member of the Newcastles of the World since its creation in 1998 and is twinned with a Swiss city, Aarau, and two European cities: Besançon in France and Sansepolcro, in Italy.

Place des Halles, Neuchâtel

The colourful roofscape of Neuchâtel, Switzerland.

Newcastle, South Africa

Newcastle is the third largest city in the province of KwaZulu-Natal, South Africa, positioned between Durban and Johannesburg, linked by rail, road and air and perfectly positioned on the Drakensberg escarpment world heritage site.

Newcastle is the third-largest city in the province with a population of 363,236 in the 2011 census. 56,144 of these citizens reside in Newcastle West, Charlestown whilst the balance of the population reside in the main townships of Madadeni, Osizweni, including the rural areas of Newcastle North, East and South.

The largest municipality within the Amajuba District, Newcastle is modern and vibrant and surrounded by beautiful hills and valleys, nature and wildlife. In addition to agriculture, tourism, coal mining and textiles, engineering is an important sector and Arcelor Mittal steel works is the second largest steel manufacturing plant in South Africa., Recent years have seen 120 new manufacturing companies, many Chinese and Taiwanese, with an investment totaling more than R1 billion ($75 million) The renovated airport creates a conducive environment for business and investors, with a Techno Hub development as a catalytic facility for innovation, creativity and research. Majuba TVET College is a nationally recognised Industry Training Centre which provides institutional skills training in all the major trade disciplines.

Infrastructure development has been a priority with a newly constructed municipal building, the Meadowlands Estate in Madadeni, Vulintaba Golf & Country Estate, Newcastle Mall and continuous roadworks to ease the traffic that comes with economic growth.

The City takes its name from the Duke of Newcastle, the secretary of the state for the British colonies when Newcastle was laid out in 1864 on the site of the drift over the Ncandu River. Newcastle was a major transport junction and popular stopover during the late 1800s, 1890 the first train arrived in Newcastle and in 1891, Newcastle was declared a borough.

Influenced by the discovery of large deposits of coal in the area the city became a centre of commercial activity, attracting ISCOR's (South African Iron and Steel Industrial Corporation Limited) steel works development in 1969.

Sir Rider Haggard, author of *King Solomon's Mines* made his home in Newcastle and his Hilldrop house is now a popular hotel among a wealth of other tourist attractions.

Top: A welcome to Newcastle, South Africa.
Right: Newcastle friends all over the world - KwaZulu-Natal.

19

Neuburg an der Donau, Germany
neuburg-donau.de

Neuburg on the Danube with its population of 30,000 inhabitants is situated in the centre of Bavaria, the southernmost state in Germany. It is about 100 kilometres (60 miles) away from the Bavarian capital city of Munich, as well as from the three other cities in Bavaria, Augsburg, Nuremberg and Regensburg.

2000 years ago the Romans had already settled on the Stadtberg, the old part of the town on a flat-topped hill. In 1214 the name of Neuburg is mentioned in a document for the first time, the so-called Pappenheimer Rent-roll.

After a war of succession between Palatinate and Bavarian members of the House of Wittelsbach, Ottheinrich became the first duke of the Platinate-Neuburg principality. For three hundred years, Ottheinrich and seven succeeding Palatine counts were to govern Neuburg through a most illustrious period. During his reign he enlarged his medieval residence into a stately palace with high Renaissance gables and a beautiful courtyard surrounded by arcades. It took on its present-day form during the reign of Duke Philipp Wilhelm, the third duke of the principality, with the addition of the Baroque eastern wing and the two round towers.

Today the Palace of Neuburg accommodates the State Gallery of Flemish Baroque Paintings with 150 works by Rubens, Van Dyck and many more of the most important Flemish artists. Situated in the east wing, there is an exhibition on the Palatinate-Neuburg Principality with interesting exhibits from this period. The shell grottos and the palace chapel with its Bocksberg frescos are unique. Together with old patrician houses and aristocrats' mansions with their superb facades, the imposing churches, the provincial library and the ancient mint, the castle still dominates the lovely Danube valley from a Jurassic limestone hill. The historic town centre boasts Baroque and Renaissance splendour at the Karlsplatz (the square in front of the town hall) which is recognised as one of the most beautiful squares in the whole of southern Germany.

In 1772, Neuburg became a garrison town and was the home of the 15th infantry regiment for ninety-one years. Its military tradition was kept alive, when after the Second World War the military airfield was rebuilt and is now the airbase and home of the Tactical Squadron 74.

When in the late forties and early fifties of the 20th century thousands of refugees came to Neuburg and settled here, not only did its population grow rapidly but it was also the beginning of the town's industrial development. A number of enterprises, like the Audi Experience Centre, employ between 400 and 1,000 workers and have guaranteed an extremely low unemployment rate in recent times.

But Neuburg is not only a good place to find a job, it can also offer people a great number of leisure time activities with widely-varied cultural programmes all year round. With the help of hundreds of volunteers, a number of sports, cultural and social clubs organise a great range of events offering an excellent quality of life.

Top: Neuburg Swimming festival.
Right: The Christmas Market
Far right: Neuburg Castle festival.

21

Neuburg an der Donau Castle, Germany. On the banks of the Danube,

New Castle, Pennsylvania, USA
newcastlepa.org

New Castle, Pennsylvania is the county seat of Lawrence County with a population of 24,000.

In 1798, John Carlysle Stewart, a civil engineer, travelled to Western Pennsylvania to resurvey the 'donation lands' granted by the government to revolutionary war veterans. In the course of performing his task, he discovered that the original survey forgot to stake out fifty acres at the confluence of the Shenango River and Neshannock Creek. Stewart claimed it for himself beginning the City of New Castle.

Stewart laid out the town and New Castle became a borough in 1825, having a population of about 300 and a city in 1869 with a population of 6,000. Business in New Castle began to flourish in the early 1800s with the construction of the canal system. Numerous manufacturing plants located in New Castle because of the availability of transport and ready access to raw material markets. The canal system was supplemented and then replaced by the railroad system.

By 1900 New Castle was one of the fastest growing cities in the country as it became the tin plate capital of the world and its population swelled to 38,280 as immigrants flocked to the city to work in the mills. In the 1920s the landscape of the city was transformed with the building of many beautiful structures, some of which still stand such as The Cathedral, St. Mary's Church, and the Castleton Hotel. The city also established its identity and New Castle is known both as the 'hot dog capital of the world' and the 'fireworks capital of America.' Its chili dogs are the product of Greek immigrants who arrived in the early 1900s and established restaurants along with their homes. The notoriety for fireworks is credited to two local fireworks companies of international stature, S.Vitale Pyrotechnic Industries, Inc. (Pyrotecnico) and Zambelli Internationale.

Over the past forty years, New Castle has been transformed from its primary reliance on industry to a well-balanced economic base comprised of manufacturing, retail and services. Many buildings and old stately homes are being restored by developers and families and the Lawrence County Historical Society, chartered in 1938, is located in the elegant nineteen-room Joseph A Clavelli mansion which overlooks the City of New Castle.

The Warner Brothers, Sam, Albert, Jack and Harry, established their first motion picture theatre in New Castle in 1907 showing the silent film *The Great Train Robbery*. Bob Hope began his solo stage career in New Castle in 1927 as part of a vaudeville production.

The City of New Castle has numerous parks within its boundaries that host many activities including those of little league baseball and adult softball leagues. Annual events such as 'Back to the 50s', are held at Cascade Park, one of the city's oldest and best known parks.

The City of New Castle has been referred to as 'Little New York City' because of its rich ethnic, religious, and racial diversity. There is even a replica of the Statue of Liberty.

Top: Swing your
partners!
Above: Scottish Rite
Cathedral

25

Nyborg, Denmark
nyborg.dk/da

Nyborg is located on the island of Funen situated at the heart of the Kingdom of Denmark. The municipality has a total population of 32,000 and the main city, Nyborg, has 16.500 inhabitants. The towns of Ørbæk and Ullerslev have populations of 2,700 and 1,600 respectively and the rest of the population live in one of the more than 20 villages of different sizes.

Nyborg is a progressive town with an active and flourishing business community and numerous hotels and conference venues only a little more than one hour by train from Copenhagen and international airports. This focus is on a on circular economy and the food sector defines the companies in Nyborg. Offering seven different secondary educations and a youth council, Nyborg is insuring the future of the community. Nyborg is among the best places in Denmark to attract visitors. Two significant events are the medieval festival the first weekend of July and the Danehof and Christmas market in the old King's Town every first and second weekend of December.

Nyborg developed as a town when Nyborg Castle, the new castle, was built around 1170. Nyborg castle is one of the most important cultural heritage monuments from medieval Denmark and one of the oldest preserved royal castles in Denmark. Nyborg was strategically located to guard the Great Belt, which gave access to the Baltic Sea and what was the Danish Baltic Sea Empire. The castle was extended by the Danish kings in the 13th century, making it a royal power base until the mid-16th century. In 1525 Nyborg was officially announced as the first real capital of the Kingdom of Denmark. It was at Nyborg Castle that, for nearly two centuries, the king met with his parliament, Danehoffet, and it was there that the kingdom's first constitution was signed in 1282 and where the foundation of the Danish parliamentary system was laid.

As part of a larger venture in Nyborg which aims to visualise and vitalise the unique cultural heritage in and around Nyborg Castle and town, the restoration of the royal castle is taking place. The plan is to restore both its original size and shape and make the preserved building accessible to the public. New buildings are to be constructed, the historical buildings are to be restored and the unique urban spaces around the castle are to be given a modern touch. Efforts are also being made to propose Nyborg as a candidate for inclusion on UNESCO's World Heritage list.

Nyborg has the world's third-longest suspension bridge linking Funen and Seeland. The sport of handball originated in Nyborg.

Top: Nyborg Castle royal
wing and moat.
Above: Christmas market in
old Royal Nyborg.

Nyborg - The Heart of the Kingdom of Denmark.

Newcastle, Australia
visitnewcastle.com.au

Newcastle, Australia's seventh-largest city with a metropolitan area population of 322,278 (2016 census), sits at the mouth of the Hunter River 160km north of Sydney.

Before European settlement, the region was home to various Aboriginal tribes, who called it Mulubinba after the name of a native fern that grew abundantly in the area. Newcastle City Council would later be recognised as the first council in Australia to raise the Aboriginal flag above its City Hall.

Royal Navy Lieutenant John Shortland became the first European to explore the area after he set off from Sydney in September, 1797 in pursuit of escaped convicts. He came across what is now called Newcastle Harbour and also the area's rich coal deposits, prompting the establishment of a new mining colony where convicts were sent to toil underground. The city's reputation as a centre for coal and other heavy industry endured until the late 20th century, when the closure of the BHP Steelworks triggered a gradual shift in focus towards education, health and hospitality.

Today, Newcastle is rapidly emerging as an innovative, smart city built on user-friendly technology and connectivity, an evolution recognised in 2017 by the Organisation for Economic Co-operation and Development. This followed the city's recognition as a United Nations City in 2016, when the University of Newcastle was made a training base to help meet the UN's global sustainability goals.

More than forty-five per cent of the city's workforce is employed in either health care, education and training, retail or the accommodation and food service industries. Mining now accounts for less than two per cent of the total workforce, but Newcastle remains home to the world's largest coal export port, handling almost 168 million tonnes of the mineral in 2016. It will always be linked to its mining past after deriving its name from England's Newcastle upon Tyne, where many of the city's 19th century coal-miners were from.

Newcastle is also one of Australia's leading regional cities of culture, with a museum, art gallery and historic theatre all within a central cultural precinct. The harbourside Honeysuckle precinct - once home to train lines and shipping berths - now features residential apartments, cafes, bars, restaurants and commercial buildings.

The city's biggest tourist attraction is arguably its spectacular coast, with five patrolled beaches, a swimming hole hewn by convicts out of the coastal rock platform and two separate ocean baths, including the biggest baths complex in the Southern Hemisphere.

Top: Newcastle's
coastline.
Above: The Newcastle
500.

Nové Hrady, Czech Republic
novehrady.cz

Nové Hrady is a town of 2,600 inhabitants in the South Bohemia Region of the Czech Republic. It is picturesquely located at the foot of the Nové Hrady (Novohradské) Mountains only 1km from the Czech-Austrian border and 30 km south-east of the regional city Czech Budejovice (České Budějovice). The town is situated above the Stropnice river that rises in the mountains and flows north to the town through the romantic nature park called Theresa's Valley ()

Nové Hrady is in a region of the country that used to be called the Sudetenland - an area once populated by millions of ethnic Germans.

The town dates back to the 13th century when a settlement developed around a castle built along a trail and trade route leading from Austria to Bohemia. This dramatic Gothic castle was therefore initially a pass-through castle with two gateways situated on a 50m high promontory and surrounded by a 14m deep moat. The castle came into the ownership of the Rožmberk family in 1358 and was subsequently damaged by military forces and natural disasters. When the Rožmberk family line died out in the early 17th century, the castle was taken over by the Count of Buquoy whose family ancestors left their mark on the town. In the late 20th century there was major restoration of the castle ('the old castle') which is now a significant tourist attraction and venue for events.

The Buquoys themselves lived in the Mansion (Rezidence – now a fine hotel) until the early 19th century when they moved to the newly-built chateau – the 'new castle'. This now houses the Institute of Physical Biology of the University of South Bohemia whose Academic and University Centre makes Nové Hrady the smallest university town in the Czech Republic.

The town has several other important cultural and historical monuments, including the church and the monastery (whose renovation in the 1990s was the work of the renowned and much-loved Father Bonfilius), the Buquoy tomb, the historic blacksmith's workshop, the tannery, city hall, the city gate fortification remains, the baroque pharmacy, and romantic and historic houses on the town square.

Having formerly been at the extremity of the 'Iron Curtain' of Communist eastern Europe, the opening of the border with Austria has created new opportunities with its neighbours for tourism and for economic and social development. The majority of people in the town and surrounding area work in agriculture, forestry and fisheries. Nové Hrady is an ideal tourist starting point for walkers, skiers and conservationists and it is also developing a network of local trails for cycling.

Throughout the year and especially during the summer tourist season, Nové Hrady holds a wide range of cultural and sporting events involving schools, civic associations, various institutions, the academic centre, and many volunteers. The town has become an attractive place for an active and full life and wins national awards for the way in which it supports and engages its older citizens.

Top: The old castle.
Behind: Tradional dancers.

Newcastle, Ontario, Canada
villageofnewcastle.ca

The Village of Newcastle in Ontario Canada resides along the shoreline of Lake Ontario in the municipality of Claringdon about an hour east of Toronto. A community rich in history, by Canadian standards, has grown into a charming village that just over 9,000 people call home. The appeal of Newcastle has made it an ideal setting for both young families and active retirees.

In 1796, Richard Lovekin came from Ireland to settle in Clarke Township near where the Village of Newcastle would one day stand. He came to an unbroken pristine wilderness. Large trees obscured the sun at midday and wild animals were plentiful. The Lovekin Family still live on their original farm. They have been on this land for 215 years having the longest tenure of a property owned by one family in Canada outside of the Province of Quebec.

The settlement of Newcastle properly began in 1833 when Stephan Crandell opened a tavern in the forest. In 1835 he was joined by Ezra Shelley who opened up a shop nearby. This little settlement became known as Crandell's Corners and about the same time another community to the south, Port Bond Head, began to grow. In 1839, work began on a pier by the Bond Head Harbour Company. The directors envisioned a large community with a busy harbour, but it never overtook Crandell's Corners, soon to be renamed Newcastle, which was strategically located on the Danforth Road (present day Ontario Highway 2). This was the main east/west thoroughfare. Also, some settlers felt the lake marshes were conducive to fever and sickness and stayed away from the lake front. In 1851 the two communities, Bond Head and Newcastle amalgamated as the Village of Newcastle. Although Bond Head retained its original name, in common usage it was referred to as Port Newcastle or Newcastle Harbour.

The Village of Newcastle has grown and matured into a vibrant community well known for its many festivals and events, farmers market and picturesque conservation areas. Apple orchards surround the town and Niagara Falls is within easy reach.

The growth of Newcastle has been dramatic and with forecasts of a doubling of the population in the next ten years, the focus is on supporting infrastructure and an increase in local businesses. This growth is paired with significant public input which ensures that the charm and history of the village are always kept in mind.

Daniel Massey was born in Newcastle in 1798 and founded a workshop to build farm implements in the town. The company eventually became the multi-national Massey-Ferguson and the original Massey building still stands in the village.

Newcastle, Ontario, Canada is a wonderful community where a smile, a wave and even sometimes a pint are a part of everyone's day.

Top: Mounties.
Top right:
Community Hall.
Above: A fine
welcome to
Newcastle, Ontario.

Jaunpils, Latvia
jaunpils.lv/municipality.php

Jaunpils, Latvia is where the medieval and modern epochs come together under the wing of the great castle.

Jaunpils County was established by the joining of Jaunpils and Viesatas Parishes on 1 July 2009 creating an area of 209 square kilometres with a population of 2,678. It is a place where one can fall in love with the silence and peace of fields, get to know the traditions and customs of the inhabitants and discover the treasures of the past.

Dominated by the 700-year old Jaunpils Castle, the cultural heritage of the area is very evident with cultural centres and a museum. There is a weaver workshop 'Dzipars', a manufacturer of peat briquettes, a cheese factory and delicious smoked products made by the local farms. The bathhouse 'Bramani' offers opportunities for steam baths and birch twig treatments and the lake of Dzirnavas is home to many graceful swans.

The main economy of the county is agricultural production. There are numerous farms and the herds of Latvian brown, black and white cows stand stately on the deep green pastures. The cattle-breeding research station was one of the first of its kind in Latvia, and it still operates successfully. Formerly it was the Livestock Breeding School (1927-1940) based in the castle.

Crops of wheat, barley, rape and corn are grown and some farms are engaged in non-traditional agriculture – biological agriculture, rural tourism, fish farming, and apiculture. The honey of Jaunpils is said to have special healing powers.

The romantic Jaunpils Castle was built in 1301 as the fortress of the Livonian Order and has remained largely intact rising proudly from the picturesque landscape and surrounded by flat hills in a circle of ponds.

The old castle of knights in Jaunpils is a place where one can still feel the breath of the Middle Ages with some medieval characters such as 'Brother Theodore, the Key Keeper' in attendance. There is a medieval pub under the vaulted ceiling where guests enjoy feasts eaten with the hands or wooden spoons in the candlelight. Every year on the second Saturday of August Jaunpils Castle hosts the Medieval Festival where the household receives foreign lords of manors, knights, palace dancers, singers and other entertainers culminating in a ball in the courtyard of the castle.

Jaunpils cultural history is tied with the name of Krisjanis Barons (best known as the 'father of the dainas' (Latvian: "Dainu tēvs") thanks largely to his systematisation of the Latvian folk songs and his work in preparing their texts for publication in Latvjan dainas. Barons was very prominent among the young Latviansas as an important writer and editor. He was born in Strutele manor and the manor territory was his family home. A primary school based in Strutele manor took the name of Krisjanis Barons for many years.

Top left and right: Castle festivities.
Middle: Jaunpils Castle.
Right: Jaunpils, a rural idyll.

Jaunpils Castle, Latvia.

New Castle, Indiana, USA
cityofnewcastle.net

Located on Interstate 70 in East Central Indiana, New Castle is 44 miles (71 km) east-northeast of Indianapolis, on the Big Blue River. The city has a population of 18,000 and is the county seat of Henry County. Together with the county, the combined population reaches 49,500.

Agriculture is the biggest industry where corn, soybeans and wheat are grown. Top livestock types include hogs, cattle, horses, sheep and lambs.

The largest employers in the New Castle area are manufacturers of projection screens, gymnasium equipment, fork lift trucks, automotive components, stainless plate, food and animal feed. In the past, New Castle was a manufacturing centre for the production of sheet iron and steel, automobiles, caskets, clothing, scales, bridges, pianos, furniture, handles, shovels, lathes, bricks, and flour. The Maxwell Automobile Factory, later owned and operated by the Chrysler Corporation was, at the time of construction in the first part of the 20th century, the largest automotive manufacturing plant in the world.

Ivy Tech Community College has a campus in New Castle, which offers associate degrees, with nursing students having the highest enrollment. Indiana University East also has a presence in the community and Ball State and Anderson Universities are located within 25 miles (40 km) of New Castle.

The city was organized administratively in 1822, plotted in 1823 and named after New Castle, Kentucky which itself was named after Newcastle upon Tyne in England. Henry County was named after the patriot and Governor of Virginia, Patrick Henry.

Henry County was the birthplace of aviator, Wilbur Wright, and is the setting for Ross Lockridge's book, *Raintree County*. Wilbur Wight Birthplace and Museum sees over 8,000 visitors each year who get a glimpse of the original *Wright Flyer*, modeled after the Smithsonian Exhibition.

After co-hosting Newcastles of the World in 2002 with New Castle Pennsylvania, the community lost their connection for a short while due to career and personnel changes. Two representatives, attended the conference in Toronto in 2016 re-connecting with Newcastles of the World. The Indiana group hopes to establish a youth organisation, promote interaction and participate in projects.

Top: Henry County court
house.
Above: Robert Indiana's
'Love' sculpture.

41

Newcastle-under-Lyme, England
newcastle-staffs.gov.uk

The loyal and ancient borough of Newcastle-under-Lyme is situated in the heart of England between Birmingham and Manchester and adjacent to Stoke-on-Trent, a city renowned the world over for its pottery industry. In 2011 the population of the borough was 128,264, the two main centres of population being Newcastle and Kidsgrove and there is now a considerable rural area within an expanded borough.

Historically, Newcastle was a market town serving a large area of North Staffordshire with some industry including brick production and felt hat manufacture. In the nineteenth century it became a major centre for coal mining and iron working, but both those industries have closed. Brick and roof tile factories still operate, and with the proximity to the M6 motorway, warehousing and distribution have taken over much of the area vacated by the coal industry. There are a number of small specialised engineering firms and Keele University, recently voted the most cost-effective place for young people to learn in the UK, located on a campus just outside the town has also attracted a number of high tech companies to its booming science park.

Newcastle developed in the 12th century round the New Castle, built to replace an earlier one at Chesterton, to the north of the town. It was granted a charter in 1173 by Henry II, and constituted a free borough by Henry III in 1235. By the 16th century the castle had vanished, apart from 'one great Toure'. Today only a mound and some stonework remain.

The name Newcastle is of obvious origin, the 'Under Lyme' is likely to have come from the Lyme Forest that stretched across this part of England. Ashton under Lyme near Manchester has the same derivation.

Newcastle has a good selection of independent local traders in its retailing heart and its historic market – which dates back to 1173 – operates six days each week. The borough is home to the New Victoria Theatre, the first purpose built theatre in the round in Europe, which offers a full programme of events throughout the year. Their Borderlines project works with disadvantaged youngsters and has connections across Europe.

Newcastle boasts two Museums, the Brampton, a local history museum with an impressive indoor street of Victorian shop fronts and Apedale Heritage site where it is possible to go down a drift coal mine.

2018 saw the 250th anniversary of the modern circus founded by Newcastle-born Phillip Astley. Arnold Bennett, writer of novels based in the Potteries, went to school in Newcastle (in his novels it is Oldcastle)

Situated in the Heart of England within easy reach of many attractions including the Peak District, Welsh Hills, Alton Towers, Chester and Chatsworth House, Newcastle makes an ideal base for touring the centre of the country.

Top: Brampton Park Museum.
Above: Newcastle's Town crier.
Above right: Queens Gardens.
Right: The historic market.

Nové Zámky, Slovakia

novezamky.sk

The town is located on the Danubian Lowland, on the Nitra River, at an altitude of 119 metres. It is a road and railway hub of southern Slovakia. The town of 38,584 people (November 2017) lies in the temperate zone and has a continental climate.

The main economic activity of Nové Zámky is agriculture with the cultivation of cereals, vegetables and oil seeds. More than sixty-nine per cetn of the cadastral area of the city is used as arable land. The vineyards around Nové Zámky provides the right conditions for grape varieties that demand heat and sunshine.

The name of the town of Nové Zámky is derived from the wooden fortification which was built on the lands of Pavol Várday, archbishop of Ostrihom in 1545 for protection against Turkish raids. This name was transferred to the later built fortress, which became the foundation of the city. The plural in the Slovak name is derived from the time when the fortresses stood next to each other.

The history of Nové Zámky is often associated with the Middle Ages, when four villages - Nyarhíd, Gúg, Györök and Lék - were located in the territory of today's Nové Zámky. The first fortress was built on the left bank of the Nitra River in 1545. The second, modern Renaissance fortress was built on the right bank of the river in 1573-1580. The new fortress was designed by Italian architects Ottavio and Giulio Baldigar with a regular hexagonal floor plan and the walls encircled by a wide moat. Nové Zámky

The main square in
Nové Zámky, Slovakia.

became the centre of anti-Turkish defence in Western Slovakia in the 16th and early 17th centuries and the castle was considered one of the best fortresses of the Habsburg monarchy.

The fortress survived several Ottoman attacks in the mid-17th century so proving its strength. The struggle for the fortress culminated in 1663 when the castle garrison was forced to surrender on 24 September. The city and surroundings suffered under Ottoman domination for twenty-two years until the imperial Habsburg army occupied the fortress on August 19, 1685 and the castle was liberated.

In 1691, archbishop Juraj Szécsényi issued a charter declaring Nové Zámky a city.

There is much for the visitor to see and do in Nové Zámky with the beautiful thermal water spas and heritage such as the catacombs under the Franciscan monastery which survived Turks, Nazis and Communists. There are concerts, feasts and festivals such as Pumpkin Day and Klobfest, a sausage making contest.

Miriam Roth, author, educationalist and scholar of , was born here in 1910.

Nové Zámky was represented at an exhibition called Spring in Newcastles 2017 in Nové Hrady. In the future, Nové Zámky plans to participate in other projects with Newcastles of the World.

Kota Bharu, Malaysia
mpkbbri.gov.my

Kota Bharu, Malaysia is the state capital and royal seat of Kelantan. The city is situated in the northeastern part of Peninsular Malaysia lying near the mouth of the Kelantan River and an hour's drive from the Thai border. With a population of 528,225 (2014) it is the largest of the Newcastles.

The city is home to many mosques, cultural activities, various museums and the unique Malay architecture of the old royal palaces. The climate is of a tropical rainforest, sunshine and rain with an average of 2,600mm of precipitation annually. Heavy rains occur during the months from October to January with slightly cooler temperatures.

Kota Bharu was established by His Royal Highness the late Sultan in 1844 as Kelantan's capital after the old capital, Kota Lama (Old Castle) which was located on the low-lying Sabak Island was destroyed by a flood. On December 8, 1941, the Japanese made Kota Bharu the first landing zone of the Malayan campaign. Taken relatively quickly it acted as an airbase for the Japanese air force as they fought the British in Malaysia and Singapore. In 1948 after the war Kota Bharu and the state of Kelantan joined the Federation of Malaya as a semi-independent British colony. At that time the city started to become more religiously conservative. When Malaysia achieved independence in 1968 after being delayed due to a Communist revolution, Kota Bharu was recognized as being a strict Islamic enclave.

Prior to this date, Kota Bharu was known as the centre of administration and business activities. The vast majority of the population is . are concentrated in urban Kota Bharu.

The elegant Sultan Ismail Petra Arches.

Kota Bharu market

Kota Bharu's population is seventy per cent Muslim with the remainder consisting mainly of Buddhists, Hindus and Christians. On 1 October 2005, Kota Bharu was declared 'Kota Bharu, The Islamic City,' a title given to the city which observes Islamic principles in every aspect of daily life. The Azan (prayer call), can be heard everywhere, even in shopping malls but the freedom of all religions still exists.

The Kelantanese culture is highly influenced by Thai culture because of its geographical proximity to Thailand. The Chinese are much more assimilated with local culture when compared with other parts of Malaysia. However the Malay culture is still prominent and Kelantan is also known as the Cradle of the Malay culture. Much of the food is sweet and spicy, with rice as the primary staple of the local diet. Traditional cultural performances of shadow puppets, drumming, top spinning and Malay martial art defence are still widely practised.

Akhaltsikhe, Georgia

Akhaltsikhe, Georgia is located in the Southern part of Georgia, a country at the intersection of Europe and Asia. The city is an economic, cultural and administrative centre of the Samtskhe-Javakheti region with a population of 17,903 (2014) and situated on the River Potskhovi.

Akhaltsikhe Branch of Ivane Javakhishvili Tbilisi State University was founded in 1990. Later on, in 2014 the University was granted the status of a higher educational institution – Samtskhe-Javakheti State University.

The city officially dates from the 11th century after the city of Lomsia was destroyed on the same site. At the beginning of the 12th century King David IV, the Builder, started to restore cities across the country and created defensive systems against Seljuk Turks. On behalf of the king`s instructions Bashqen II Jaqeli re-built the castle naming it Akhaltsikhe or 'new castle.'

Archeological excavations have confirmed that the third millennium terraced settlement existed on the Amirani hill, where tombs, utility structures, metal and ceramic tools were found. Primitive wood and leather processing tools from the Stone Age were also discovered.

In 1576, the Ottomans took the city and from 1628 the city became the centre of the Samtskhe Eyalet of the Ottoman Empire as 'Ahıska'. In 1828, during the Russo-Turkish War of 1828–1829, Russian troops under the command of General Paskevich captured the city and, as a consequence of the 1829 Treaty of Adrianople (Edirne), it was ceded to the Russian Empire as part of first Kutaisi and then Tiflis Governorates.

In the late 1980s the city was host to the Soviet Army's 10th Guards Motor Rifle Division, which became a brigade of the Georgian land forces after the fall of the Soviet Union and independence of Georgia in 1991.

Akhaltsikhe (Rabati) castle complex covers seven hectares. The castle was surrounded by three lines of walls, including gates and watch-towers and connected to the suburbs of the town via tunnels. The castle was restored in 2012 and became an important historical and tourist centre. The contrast of the old castle and modern infrastructure, cafes, hotels, shops make the castle an attractive place to visit.

Saint Shalva of Akhaltsikhe was a Georgian public figure and military leader of the 12th-13th Centuries and saint of the Orthodox church. He is celebrated on June 30 with a major festival.

On June 30, 2017 twelve young performers from Newcastle, South Africa and eight from Newcastle upon Tyne, UK accepted the invitation from the Mayor of Akhaltsikhe to visit the country and appear at the annual St Shalva Day cultural festival. It was a great opportunity to exchange culture and traditions and guests had a chance to visit the most important sights of the Samtskhe-Javakheti region.

Top: Music and festivities
at Akhaltsikhe.
Above: Akhaltsikhe Castle.

49

Other Newcastles

UK and Eire

Newcastle on Clun, England

Newcastle on Clun is a rural village of 300 people situated at the head of the Clun Valley in Shropshire five miles east (8km) of the border with Wales. The village is on the West side of Offa's Dyke and through the centuries has alternated between the two countries. The name of the village derives from the Roman fort, Novum Castrum which sits on Vron Hill overlooking the settlement.

Newcastle is a livestock producing district and in a designated Area of Outstanding Natural Beauty with many hiking trails. The nearby Clun Forest is a former royal hunting forest and the 400-year old Moor Hall still boasts a spear rack for huntsmen. Until 1962 an inland lighthouse existed to guide the huntsmen home.

Newcastle, Emlyn, Wales

Newcastle Emlyn is a town of 1,200 people of whom approximately half are Welsh-speaking. It grew up as a crossing point of the River Teifi for cattle drovers and the town still boasts a dairy industry with a mozzarella cheese factory.

The town's ruined Norman castle has a legend of the last dragon in Wales attached to it. It tells how a winged, fire-breathing viper called a 'wyvern' landed on the walls and brought terror to the town. It was lured to its death by a soldier, Rhys of Flendre, who floated a red cloak in the river and shot the beast from below as it fell upon the cloak. In its death throes it bled venom into the river and poisoned all the fish.

Peter Rees Jones, founder of the Peter Jones London department store, was born in Newcastle, Emlyn in 1843.

Newcastle, Emlyn, Wales.

Newcastle, Monmouth, Wales

A tiny hamlet five miles (8 km) north of Monmouth, Newcastle, or Castell-newydd in Welsh, has a Norman motte and bailey castle site from which its name is derived. The bailey is defended by a banked ditch but the oval motte and surrounding wet ditch now have farm buildings encroaching. It commands impressive views to the West towards the River Trothy valley.

Newcastle, County Down, Northern Ireland

Newcastle, County Down is situated on the coast and immortalised in the song by Percy French as the place 'where the Mountains of Mourne sweep down to the sea.' It has a population of 7,500 and is famed for the Royal County Down Golf Club which has one of the finest golf courses in the world.

Newcastle takes its name from the 'new castle' built in 1588 to replace an older fortification and the town grew up around it with fishing being an important industry. In 1820 Lord Annersley built a pier in Newcastle Harbour as a loading point for Mourne granite. The castle was demolished in 1830. In 1843 a major fishing disaster claimed the lives of forty-six Newcastle men leaving twenty-seven widows, 118 children and twenty-one other dependents. A street of cottages, Widows' Row, was built and funded by public subscription for the widows and dependants and a local song about the disaster says 'Newcastle town is one long street entirely stripped of men.'

Florence Balcombe, wife and literary executor of Bram Stoker, author of *Dracula*, was born in Newcastle in 1858.

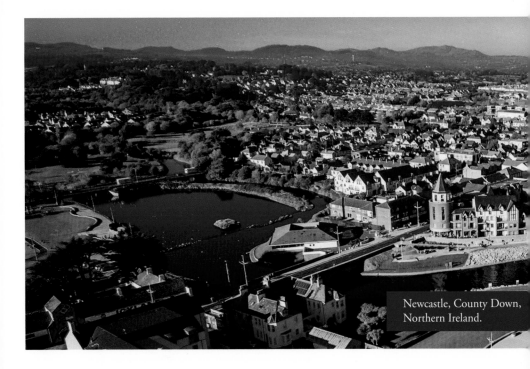

Newcastle, County Down, Northern Ireland.

Newcastleton, Scotland

visitnewcastleton.com

Situated in the Scottish Borders in an area known as Liddesdale, Newcastleton has a population of 850 and is also known locally as Copshaw Holm or simply the Holm. It is surrounded by fabulous scenery of hills and forests and is popular with visitors who come to mountain bike, walk, golf and fish.

The Borders area was once one of conflict from the time of the Romans in the 1st century, through the invasion of the Normans and then the constant battles between the Scots and the English. In the 12th century the strongholds of Hermitage Castle and Liddel Castle were built in Liddelsdale and the ruins of Liddel Castle remain. The lands of Castleton held the church, the castle demesne and formed the core of the valley in medieval times but it was not until 1793 that the town of Castleton was built by Henry, 3rd Duke of Buccleugh to a well-planned and regular lay-out.

Newcastle West, Eire

visitnewcastlewest.ie

Newcastle West is the capital town of County Limerick in the West of Ireland with a population of 6,600. Its Irish name is Caislean Nua Thiar. The stone castle, seat of the Earl of Desmond, was completed in 1298, the ruins of which are located off the town square. The town then came to be known as Newcastle, West Limerick, but over time it has become known as Newcastle West.

The town has a violent history being sacked in 1302 and destroyed in 1315. During the reign of Elizabeth I in the 16th century three battles were fought nearby and tradition has it that many of the Knights Templar as well as two Earls of Desmond were killed here.

Newcastle, Wicklow, Eire

visitwicklow.ie

Newcastle, Wicklow is situated in the east of Ireland about 28 miles (45 km) south of Dublin City. It has a population of 950 and takes its name from the Norman Castle, now a ruin, built by Hugh de Lacy, governor of Ireland under Henry II, between 1177 and 1184. It was attacked at intervals by the Irish chieftains, the O'Tooles and the O'Byrnes.

Newcastle was once the major administrative and judicial centre of Wicklow in the 13th and 14th Centuries but by the beginning of the 19th century had declined to a small village. Today it is picturesque and close to the beach which is popular with walkers and fishermen.

Newcastle, Galway, Eire

Newcastle, Galway, has now been absorbed into the City of Galway but in the past was outside the City walls and the home of a famous clan, the O'Flaherties who had been expelled from the City by the ruling Burgo family.

Nothing remains of the 'new castle' but the ruins of the old castle are still visible. The

Persse family owned a whiskey distillery and took the stone from the new castle to build a house.

Newcastle houses Galway's cathedral, opened in 1963 and much of the university and has a population of 7,000.

North America

Newcastle, Washington State, USA
newcastlewa.gov

The Pacific Northwest city of Newcastle, Washington, combines the convenience of urban living with the comfort and community of a small town. Conveniently situated near the headquarters of businesses like Amazon, Costco, Microsoft and T-Mobile, Newcastle's central location gives residents the chance to easily commute to work and return home to a small community with opportunities for outdoor recreation.

Incorporated in 1994, Newcastle is a relatively young city with a deep-rooted history. In the 1800s, Newcastle was a coal mining company town named after the famous English coal city. It became one of the most successful coal mining towns in north western Washington. The area's coal fuelled the economic growth of Seattle until the industry declined and the last mine was closed in 1963. Rusted equipment and mining shafts are still visible along Newcastle trails. Landmarks including the historic cemetery where miners are buried, and the Pacific Coast Coal Company House No. 75, a company house known as the Baima House, are tangible reminders of the past. Constructed in 1880, the house is one of the oldest buildings in the county.

Newcastle, Washington. In the Fall.

Around thirty years after the end of the coal mining era, a successful citizen effort toward incorporation established the City of Newcastle. Today, Newcastle is made up of more than 11,500 people, and is recognised as one of the best places to live in the United States. The city is also home to the Golf Club at Newcastle, which offers world class golfing and stunning, panoramic views of Seattle. Newcastle is known for its close proximity to nature, highlighted by nearly forty acres of developed parks and a vast network of trails for people to explore.

New Castle, Colorado USA

newcastlecolorado.org

As a coal mining town, New Castle, Colorado, was named after Newcastle upon Tyne. The town was established in 1888, shortly after the opening of the coal mines, and by 1898 the population had grown to 1800.

The original occupants were a band of Ute Indians, who wintered in the Colorado River and Elk Creek valleys. Jasper Ward is recognised as the first homesteader. In 1896, the Vulcan Mine exploded, killing forty-nine miners. There were further explosions in 1913 and 1918, effectively closing the mines. A downtown memorial honours the victims.

New Castle's coal is located in the Grand Hogback monocline, which crosses the Colorado River at New Castle and marks the western edge of the Rocky Mountains. Mt. Mederis rises in the middle of the town. The town's official elevation is 5,550 feet.

Like other Western Colorado towns, New Castle places a high value on outdoor recreation. The town boasts fifteen parks, a golf course and miles of hiking and mountain biking trails. The Town sponsors events throughout the year, and the largest, the Burning Mountain Festival, attracts visitors every September.

New development began to boost New Castle's population at beginning of the 1990s. In 2018 there were approximately 4,600 residents, who continue to appreciate the joys of living in a small mountain town.

New Castle, New York, USA

New Castle, New York, a town in Westchester County (18,000), was originally inhabited by several Native American tribes, and later settled by Quakers. The most renowned area and hamlet of New Castle is Chappaqua. Both Chappaqua and New Castle became well known as the residence of famous newspaper proprietor and presidential candidate Horace Greeley. More recently, Chappaqua and the Town of New Castle have attracted national attention as the home of Former U.S. President Bill Clinton and Former Secretary of State Hillary Clinton.

Nearby is New Cassel, an unincorporated place in Nassau County (14,000). Nassau County is directly east of New York City limits and therefore also within the New York metropolitan area.

Other places in North America that are officially designated as cities are: Newcastle, Oklahoma, the largest city in McClain County, part of the Oklahoma City Metropolitan Area (8,000); New Castle, an historic city in New Castle County, Delaware (5,000); Newcastle, Wyoming, a city located in Weston County (3,500); New Castle, Kentucky, a city in Henry County (900) and Newcastle, Texas, a city in Young County (600)

Other towns, townships, villages, boroughs or unincorporated communities are: Newcastle, Maine, a town in Lincoln County (1,750) - together with the village of Damariscotta linked by the Main Street bridge, it forms the "Twin Villages"; Newcastle, California, an unincorporated town in Placer County in the foothills of the Sierra Nevada mountains (1,200); New Castle, New Hampshire, a town in Rockingham County (1,000); Newcastle Township, Dixon County, Nebraska, (500).

Newcastle Township, Coshocton County, Ohio, is one of the twenty-two townships of Coshocton County (475) and includes New Castle, Ohio, an unincorporated community in Belmont County and Newcastle, Ohio, an unincorporated community in Coshocton County.

South New Castle, Pennsylvania, is a borough in Lawrence County on the southern boundary of New Castle itself (800). New Castle Township, Schuylkill County, Pennsylvania, is a township in Schuylkill County (400). Newcastle, Nebraska is a village in Dixon County (300); Newcastle, Utah, an unincorporated community in southwestern Iron County (250) and finally New Castle, in the state of Virginia, the only town in Craig County (180).

Left: Ute Native Americans.

Newcastle, Jamaica

visitjamaica.com

Newcastle Hill Station is situated in the Blue Mountains of Jamaica in the Eastern parish of St Andrew, roughly 4,000 feet above sea level and 20 miles (32 km) from Kingston on the Buff Bay Road. Formerly a British Army military barracks it is now a training centre for the Jamaican Defence Force.

The settlement's military history dates back to 1840 when Major General Sir William Maynard Gomm arrived in Jamaica as Lieutenant Governor and found that yellow fever was claiming the lives of many British troops stationed in the plains around Kingston. He noted that the disease was far less prevalent in the mountains and in 1842, after much resistance from his superiors, established a barracks at the Newcastle coffee plantation high in the cooler climate of the mountains. The death toll was dramatically reduced and the parade ground still bears Major General Gomm's name.

When Jamaica achieved independence from the British in 1962, the Jamaican Defence Force became the keeper of the Newcastle Hill Station.

Today, Newcastle is part of the Blue Mountain and John Crow Mountain National Park and surrounded by coffee plantations, vegetable farms and hiking trails which provide the main income for the 1,500-strong population of Newcastle and surrounding districts.

Newcastle
Hill Station,
Jamaica.

Newcastle, Nevis, West Indies

nevisisland.com

Newcastle, Nevis is part of the two-island country of St Kitts and Nevis lying in the northern part of the Leeward Islands group of the Lesser Antilles in the Eastern Caribbean. The two islands are separated by a channel some 3 km in width.

St Kitts and Nevis is a British constitutional monarchy, recognising Queen Elizabeth II as head of state. She is represented by a Governor-General who takes advice from the Prime Minister and cabinet.

The almost circular island of Nevis to the south-east has beaches of silver sand and coconut groves, and rises to a central peak (Mt Nevis, 985 metres) which is usually capped with white clouds. Nevis has its own legislature, Premier and administration with a population of 12,000.

Newcastle village is on the north coast of Nevis to the east of the airport, which takes its name, and at one time was an important shipping port with significant Georgian architecture. Today most of the heritage buildings have gone falling victim to airport development.

St Kitts and Nevis was virtually a sugar monocrop economy until the late 1970s, when the government backed a drive into small-scale industrialisation. Tourism has become the largest source of foreign exchange. From 1984 a small offshore sector on Nevis grew rapidly, with around 18,000 companies registered.

Newcastle, Nevis, West Indies.

Neufchâteau, France

Neufchâteau is a commune (municipality) in the Vosges department in Grand Est (formerly Lorraine region) in north eastern France.

Positioned at the confluence of the Rivers Meuse and Mouzon, the town dominates the Vosges Plain, and is on the main railway line connecting with Metz, Nancy, Dijon, Lyon and south.

One of the oldest towns in Grand Est, Neufchâteau was known as Noviomagus during the Roman period, when it was a market town along the Pretorian road connecting Lyon with Trier. The town became Novum Castrum by 1094 when Thierry, son of the Duke Gérard I constructed a castle here, and it grew in the Middle Ages thanks to the cloth trade.

Its urban landscape, developed between the 12th and 15th centuries, is dominated by major buildings such as the Saint-Christophe and Saint-Nicolas churches, but includes later mansions and bourgeois houses of the sixteenth, seventeenth and eighteenth. Its heart is the Place Jeanne d'Arc, named after the martyr Saint Joan, the 'The Maid of Orléans' who was born close by in Domrémy-la-Pucelle, part of the arrondissement (administrative district) of Neufchâteau.

In 2017, the town was recognised among the 'One-hundred most beautiful detours of France,' one of the small towns that make the charm and diversity of French tourism, usually a little off the main travel routes.

The town was represented at the very first 'Newcastles of the World' summit in Shinshiro, Japan in 1998.

Neufchâteau, France

Italy

There are twenty-two communes or municipalities called Castelnuovo in Italy and a further six smaller hamlets. In addition there are four communes called Castelnovo.

The largest is Castelnuovo Rangone (population 13,800) in the Province of Modena, part of the Emilia-Romagna region; it is located about 40 kilometres (25 miles) west of the city of Bologna and about 13 kilometres (8 miles) south of the city of Modena, and is a very important centre for the production and treatment of pork.

Others with a population of over 10,000 are:

Castelnuovo Rangone, Italy is famous for its pork.

Castelnuovo del Garda, Province of Verona, Veneto region (12,500), close to Lake Garda; in 1848 the town was almost totally destroyed and burned by the Austrian empire army (including the church and the medieval tower), during the first Italian independence war.

Castelnovo ne' Monti, Province of Reggio Emilia, Emilio Romagna region in the Apenines, central Italy (10,500); it is best known for the Pietra di Bismantova spur (literally 'Rock of Bismantova') which can be seen from a distance of 30 kilometres (19 mi) as it stands at around 1,047 metres (3,435 ft) above sea level. The rock was mentioned by the Italian poet Dante Alighieri in *The Divine Comedy*.

Between 1,000 and 10,000 population:

Castelnuovo Berardenga in the Province of Siena, Tuscany (9,000)
Castelnovo di Sotto, Province of Reggio Emilia, Emilio Romagna region (8,500)
Castelnuovo Magra, Province of La Spezia (8,500), Liguria region
Castelnuovo di Porto, Province of Rome in the region of Latium. (8,500),
Castelnuovo di Garfagnana, Province of Lucca, Tuscany (6,000)
Castelnuovo Scrivia, Province of Alessandria, region of Piedmont (5,500)
Castelnuovo Don Bosco, Province of Asti, region of Piedmont (3,200)
Castelnovo Bariano, Province of Rovigo, Veneto region (3,000)
Castelnuovo Cilento, Province of Salerno, Campania region (2,600)
Castelnuovo di Val di Cecina, Province of Pisa, Tuscany (2,300)
Castelnuovo della Daunia, Province of Foggia, Apulia region (1,400)
Castelnuovo di Conza, Province of Salerno, Campania region (1,000)
Castelnuovo di Farfa, Province of Rieti, Latium region. (1,000)

Smaller communes or hamlets of under 1,000 inhabitants are:

Castelnuovo Trentino, Province of Trento (900); Castelnuovo Belbo, Province of Asti
(900); Castelnuovo Bocca d'Adda, Province of Lodi (700); Castelnuovo Bormida,
Province of Alessandria (700); Castelnuovo Bozzente, Province of Como (800);
Castelnuovo Calcea, Province of Asti (800); Castelnuovo Nigra, Province of Turin (400);
Castelnuovo Parano, Province of Frosinone (900); Castelnuovo di Ceva, Province of
Cuneo (130); Castelnovo del Friuli, Province of Pordenone (900); Castelnuovo,
Avezzano, medieval town, Province of L'Aquila (200); Castelnuovo (Assisi), Province of
Perugia (750); Castelnuovo (Auditore), Province of Pesaro and Urbino (10); Castelnuovo
della Misericordia, Province of Livorno (165); Castelnuovo (Prato), Province of Prato
(420); Castelnuovo (Vergato), Province of Bologna (10); Castelnuovo (Teolo), part of
Teolo, Province of Padova (50)

Castelnuovo
Rangone, Italy.

Gherla, Romania
gherlainfo.ro

The city of Gherla, in the north of Romania, has a population of over 20,000. Its downtown is little changed since it was first laid out in the 18th century by a community of Armenians who settled in Transylvania after fleeing invading Tatars - though the city goes back to the 13th century. The Armenian settlers built the centre in a grid style (ahead of New York) with four straight and parallel streets intersecting at right angles, all opening to the River Somes. There is a large central square, numerous monumental baroque buildings (with

Gherla Cathedral, Romania

churches of many denominations) and an older area of winding streets to the north. The 'castle' is built on the site of an older version from the 16th century and became notorious as a prison where many political prisoners were held during Communist times.

There is also a very large park of forty hectares in the English style which contains statues of major Romanian cultural figures. It is also known as 'The Little Schönbrun' and was considered to be one of Europe's pearls as it was in the same style that was fashionable in Vienna and other parts of the Habsburg Empire. At the park entrance is a statue on a column of the Lupa Capitolina - like the one in Rome, reminding everyone that 'Romania' has its Roman heritage. The municipality's economy is dominated by the tertiary sector (services), followed by industry and also by agricultural activities. The main industrial products manufactured in the city are furniture and wood products, milling and bakery products, meat and meat products, ceramic products for construction, carpentry of wood and plastic products, textile and leather garments. There is a major dependence on the wood processing industry, which covers more than half the city's industrial production and sixty per cent of the workforce employed.

Herceg Novi, Montenegro

Herceg Novi is a coastal town in Montenegro situated at the foot of Mount Orjen and at the entrance to the beautiful and dramatic Bay of Kotor, the southernmost fjord in Europe and the deepest in the Mediterranean.

It is one of the youngest cities on the Adriatic, formerly part of the Ottoman Empire and the Republic of Venice and its history of varied occupations has created a blend of diverse and picturesque architectural styles

Herceg Novi is the administrative, economic and cultural centre of the municipality bordering Croatia and Serbia with 16,000 of the municipality's 32,000 population living in the city.

It is called 'Sun City' because of its vegetation, sun and culture. Other Mediterranean cities might be lively only in summer, but Herceg Novi is lively all year round and has another reputation as a city of award-winning festivals and cultural events. The oldest event, the annual Mimosa festival, is a winner of the international 'Golden Heart' for best tourism award.

Tourism is at the heart of the city's economy. The city is developing eco-tourism, sport tourism (including winter sports) and conferences, with attractions of gastronomy, wine, and the varied plant and animal species. There is capacity of around 6,000 hotel beds and twenty campsites with capacity for over 600 vehicles.

The main attractions are Castle Forte Mare built in 1382, the clock tower from the 19th century, the Kanli tower built by the Turks, and the Serbian church of St. Michael Archangel.

Industry is of relatively low importance, with a small industrial/storage zone and a shipyard in Bijela, the largest maintenance and repair shipyard dock in Montenegro.

Herceg Novi is less than 25km from two international airports.

The city is part of a Fraternity Charter with eleven municipalities, and it also has fourteen 'friends' municipalities, so has been active in fostering international cooperation.

Kaštel Novi, Croatia

Kaštel Novi is one of the seven Mediterranean communities within the administrative area which bear the name Kaštela on the Bay of Kaštela in Croatia, located northwest of the city of Split on the central Dalmatian coast. The municipality has 40,000 inhabitants but the town of Kaštel Novi itself has around 6,500 people.

Traces of all historic periods can be found in the area; cavemen hunted here; there are many Illyrian stone heaps scattered over the Kozjak Mountain; and during the Greek and Roman rule these parts experienced economic and cultural prosperity.

Aristocrats and clergymen from Trogir and Split built their castles on the rocky shores. Around sixteen castles seven villages were formed which grew, developed and finally merged to form the town of Kaštela. The villages preserved authentic Dalmatian architecture: houses with open front stairs, balconies, wine cellars, narrow streets and squares at their centres.

Agriculture with the growing of olives and grapes are the basis of the economy. There are large churches with bell towers (decorated by the most famous artists of the time), golden and silver gifts in church treasuries and folk costumes noted for their golden decorations and golden embroidery

In Kaštel Novi, the castle was built in 1512 in form of a rectangular keep and the settlement developed around the castle, encircled by defensive walls to the east, north and west and by the sea on the south. The parish church of St. Petar od Klobučca was built on the foundations of a church from the 13th century. It keeps a rich treasury of silver and church robes.

In the fields above Kaštel Novi vineyards were cultivated from ancient times. Only a few old species are left, but among them Crljenak kaštelanski, which is known throughout the world and especially in California as Zinfandel. The homeland of the American vine is Kaštel Novi where some vines still grow.

Kaštel Novi, Croatia

Novohrad-Volynski, Ukraine

Novohrad-Volynski (population 56,000) is at the confluence of the Sluch and Smilka rivers in the western part of Zhytomyr region of northern Ukraine. This locates it at the crossroads connecting the capital of Ukraine (Kyiv - 200km to the east) with the cities of Western Europe. The city is known for its picturesque landscapes, narrow streets, centuries-old forests and rocky banks above the river.

The history of the city extends from the earliest times and there have been archaeological finds from the stone, copper and bronze ages. The early tribes built fortified settlements which were in hard-to-reach enemy locations on the high banks of rivers, artificially reinforced with moats and shafts.

Before the annexation in 1795 of the territories of the Polish-Lithuanian Commonwealth by the Russian Empire after the third Partition of Poland, the city was known as Zvyahel. The name was mentioned first in the 13th century and became a prosperous city and a centre of craftsmanship. The town was well-fortified, enclosed by a moat, and with a castle located on the border of the high coastal plateau on the rock on the left bank of the river. The city was left with the ruins of its 14th century castle but some sections have been restored.

The city had an important Jewish community which numbered over 10,000 at the start of the 20th century; thousands died both in the pogroms of 1918/1919 and during the Second World War.

During the reconstruction and socialist construction after the Great Patriotic War of the Soviet Union (1941-45), many residential buildings, new industrial enterprises and social facilities were built and the city became an important centre for textiles, meat-packing, the wood industry, chemicals/petro-chemicals, agricultural machinery and mechanical engineering. Investors from Germany, Poland, Romania, Belgium, Turkey, Russia, Estonia and Hungary have all been active in the city in recent times

Novograd-Volynsky boasts many prominent figures in literature, culture and politics but is best known as the birthplace of Lesya Ukrainka (1871-1913), the most famous nationalist Ukrainian writer.

The view from Sluch River from castle remains. Novohrad-Volynski, Ukraine

Hoskote, India

Hoskote (sometimes called Hosakote) is a taluk (administrative district) in Bengaluru Rural District in the state of Karnataka in south west India, 30km from Bangalore, with headquarters in Hoskote town, population 57,000. Hoskote is the largest taluk in Karnataka having 333 villages.

Agriculture, apiculture (bee-keeping) and horticulture are the primary occupations of local people although industrialisation in recent times in Hoskote and surrounding areas has thrown up new opportunities.

Hoskote was a pre-historic centre but the settlement was founded by Thamme Gowda, the chief of Sugatur whose successors ruled till 1638. It later became part of Sira Province. In 1756, Hoskote was taken by the Mysore army but was subdued by the Marathas (Peshwa). It changed hands several times until it was finally annexed by Haider Ali in 1761 and then became involved in the Anglo-Mysore Wars

The old fort area, which was constructed to defend the town, has the well-known Avimukteshwara, Varadaraja and Vithoba temples, and Kote Anjaneyaswamy temple is about 800 years old but there are many other temples and shrines.

Hoskote is an important destination for birdwatchers and parasailers (a large dried lake-bed is used for the purpose).

The town lies at the intersection of the major roads NH-4 and NH-207 and as such is a busy town with both a resident and a floating population. The town has a medical college and research institute known as MVJ Medical College & Research Centre. It also has a department of the Indian Institute of Astrophysics Astrophysicists, supporting work for the world's most advanced highest altitude Thirty Metre Telescope (TMT) in India, a general-purpose observatory capable of investigating a broad range of astrophysical problems.

The annual Karaga (folk dance festival performed on a full moon day) and the Avimukteshwara Jatre (part religious procession, part cultural festival) attract thousands of people.

Hoskote
Temple, India

Map labels:
SHINSHIRO CITY, Japan
KOTA BHARU, Malaysia
NEWCASTLE, Australia
NEWCASTLE, South Africa
AKHALTSIKHE, Georgia
NOVÉ ZÁMKY, Slovakia
NOVÉ HRADY, Czech Republic
JAUNPILS, Latvia
NYBORG, Denmark
NEWCASTLE UPON TYNE, UK
NEWCASTLE-UNDER-LYME, UK
NEW CASTLE, Ontario, Canada
NEW CASTLE, Pennsylvania, USA
NEUCHÂTEL, Switzerland
NEUBURG AN DER DONAU, Germany
NEW CASTLE, Indiana, USA

'Newcastles of the World' Partner Towns and Cities (shown on map)

Shinshiro City, Japan
Newcastle, Kwazulu Natal
 South Africa
Neuburg-an-der-Donau,
 Germany
Neuchâtel, Switzerland
Newcastle-under-Lyme,
 United Kingdom
New Castle, Indiana, Uni▎
 States of America
New Castle, Pennsylvania,
 United States of America
Jaunpils, Latvia
Akhaltsikhe, Georgia
Nové Hrady, Czech Repub▎
Nyborg, Denmark
Kota Bharu, Malaysia
Newcastle, Clarington,
 Ontario, Canada
Newcastle, New South
 Wales, Australia
Nové Zámky, Slovakia
Newcastle upon Tyne,
 United Kingdom

Other Newcastles Around T
 World

EUROPE

Montenegro
Herceg Novi
Poland
Nowy Zamek
Romania
Gherla
Neufchâteau
Belgium
Portugal
Castelo Novo
Ukraine
Novohrad-Volynskyi
Spain
Castillo-Neuvo
Austria
Neuberg im Burgenland

Greece
Neokastro, Central
  Macedonia
France
Neufchâteyour (Lorraine)
Neufchateau, Châteauneuf-du-
Faou
Italy
Castelnovo Bariano
Castelnuovo Belbi
Castelnuovo Berardenga
Castelnuovo Bozzente
Castelnovo del Fruili
Castelnovo Di Sotto
Castelnovo Ne'Monti
Castelnovo (Trento)
Castelnuovo Bocca D'Adda
Castelnuovo Bormida
Castelnuovo Calcea
Castelnuovo Cilento
Castelnuovo del Garda
Castelnuova della Daunia
Castelnuovo di Ceva
Castelnuovo di Conza
Castelnuovo Di Farfa
Castelnuovo di Garfagnana
Castelnuovo di Porto
Castlenuovo Rangone, Italy
Castelnuovo di Val di Cecina
Castelnuovo don Bosco
Castlenuovo Magra
Castlenuovo Nigra
Castelnuovo Parano
Castelnuovo Scrivia
Castelnuovo Bormida
Castelnuovo Avezzano
Castelnuovo Assisi
Castelnuovo della
  Misericordia
Castelnuovo Prato
Castelnuovo Vergato
Castelnuovo Teolo
Castelnuovo Auditore
Republic of Ireland
Newcastle West , County
  Limerick in place
Newcastle, County Dublin ,
  town in South County
  Dublin
Newcastle, County Galway
Newcastle, County Tipperary
Newcastle, County Wicklow ,
  town in County Wicklow
Newcastle, Oldcastle, County
  Meath
England
Newcastle, Herefordshire

Newcastle, Shropshire
  (Newcastle on Clun), town in
  the district of South
  Shropshire
Wales
Little Newcastle (Casnewydd-
  Bach), Pembrokeshire
Newcastle, Bridgend ,
  Glamorgan
Newcastle Emlyn , Ceredigion
  place between
  (Cardiganshire) and
  Carmarthenshire
Newcastle, Monmouthshire ,
  town in Monmouthshire
Scotland
Newcastleton
Northern Ireland - *Newcastle,*
  County Down

USA
New Castle, Alabama,
  Jefferson County
Newcastle, Arkansas, Johnson
  Township
Newcastle, California, city in
  Placer County
New Castle, Colorado, in
  Garfield County
  Municipality
New Castle Hundred, a
  unified district in New Castle
  County, Delaware
New Castle, Delaware, city of
  New Castle County - and
  County of New Castle
New Castle, Illinois, Carrier
  Mills Township
New Castle, Kentucky, city in
  Henry County
Newcastle, Maine, town in
  Lincoln County - part of
  Damariscotta-Newcastle
New Castle, Missouri, Jefferson
  Township
Newcastle, Nebraska , city in
  Dixon County
New Castle, New Hampshire ,
  city in Rockingham County
New Castle, New York , town
  in Westchester County
Newcastle Township,
  Coshocton County, Ohio, city
  in Coshocton County
New Castle, Ohio, Belmont
  County
Newcastle, Oklahoma, city in

McClain County
New Castle, North Carolina,
  Wilkes County
New Castle Township,
  Pennsylvania, in Schuylkill
  County town
South Newcastle,
  Pennsylvania, Lawrence
  County
Newcastle, Texas, city in Young
  County
Newcastle, Utah, a unified
  district in Iron County
New Castle, Virginia, town in
  Craig County
Newcastle, Washington State,
  city in King County
Newcastle, Wyoming, city in
  Weston County

Canada
Newcastle, New Brunswick , a
  district in the Canadian city
  Miramichi

Jamaica
Newcastle
Barbados
Newcastle
Saint Kitts and Nevis
Newcastle
India
Hoskote
Brazil
Castello Novo
Australia
  Newcastle Waters, Northern
  Territory
Newcastle Range, Queensland

Formerly known as
  'Newcastle'
Pylos, Greece
Savonlinna, Finland
Toodyay, Western Australia,
  previously known as
  Newcastle
Casnewydd-ar-Wysg (literally,
  'Newcastle-on-Usk'), Welsh
  name for Newport
Cowichan-Newcastle , a
  former constituency in the
  Canadian province of British
  Columbia
Albert Town, Otago, New
  Zealand

Newcastles of the Network

There are currently sixteen Newcastles who are regarded as partners of the Newcastles of the World network supported by a secretariat based in Newcastle upon Tyne.

A conference is held every two years in one of the member Newcastles with a specific theme for presentations and debate. In 2014 a charter for the network was agreed and is at Appendix I.

The network's website is newcastlesoftheworld.com where further information about Newcastles and their activities can be found. A quarterly newsletter is produced and applications to join the mailing list are welcome.

Other Newcastles may apply to join the network and an application form can be obtained through the network website. A copy is at Appendix II.

Newcastles Forum – helping us connect

The Newcastles Forum is for us all to keep in touch and share news and ideas. There are sections by country, by projects, by topics of shared interest and for youth. This can be found at newcastlesforum.com or through the main website.

David Faulkner, Coordinator,
Newcastles of the World.

Young People of the Newcastles

The network has special activities for young people and a youth programme is included at every conference. This has led to a number of exchange programmes and youth projects often through the youth assemblies which exist in many of the Newcastles. In December 2017 the first exclusively youth conference took place in Shinshiro.

There is a Youth Section on the main website.

Zelie Guerin, Project Manager,
Newcastles of the World.

The sixteen Newcastle's of the World network.

The Conferences

1998 Shinshiro, Japan

In the early 1990s, Shinshiro's Mayor, Yoshio Yamamoto, travelled the world looking for a suitable sister city. He settled on the Pennsylvania city of New Castle in the USA, but then went one step further by inviting representatives of several other Newcastles to come together in Shinshiro in 1998. The idea was to exchange ideas and experiences and see if they could find opportunities to work together in an international alliance of towns and cities with the same name.

As well as the hosts and New Castle Pennsylvania, the summit was attended by representatives from Neuchâtel (Switzerland), Neufchâteau (France), Neuburg an der Donau (Germany), Newcastle Municipality (South Africa), Newcastle-under-Lyme, United Kingdom, and New Castle, Indiana, USA. Economic development was the focus of that summit, and it was a great success. 'I felt like I was at the United Nations,' recalled Tim Fulkerson, Mayor of New Castle, Pennsylvania 'We had the earphones on, with the translators speaking.'

2000 Neuchâtel, Switzerland

Promoting interchange between the Newcastles in culture, education and tourism was the theme for the second summit two years later in Neuchâtel – and it just happened

The first Newcastles conference, Shinshiro, Japan, 1998.

to coincide with the host city's big wine festival! The two American New Castles again attended as did Shinshiro, Neuburg and Newcastle-under-Lyme.

2002 The USA

When the Newcastles next met in the United States, Newcastle South Africa was back in attendance and a representative from Newcastle upon Tyne, United Kingdom attended for the first time. The summit was co-hosted by the New Castles of Indiana and Pennsylvania, with three days in each city. The main topic for the conference was how to manage the environmental challenges of the day.

Youth delegates in national dress at Newcastle, Canada, 2016.

2004 Newcastle, South Africa

The next gathering was in South Africa and the eight Newcastles that attended were the eight who were at the first conference minus Neufchâteau but including Newcastle upon Tyne. The twin themes were education and culture, and the scope for cooperation between the Newcastles in these fields.

2006 Newcastle-under-Lyme, UK

The same eight Newcastles were represented in Newcastle-under-Lyme in 2006 when the summit shared experience of how the different local councils engage with the communities they serve.

2008 Neuburg an der Donau, Germany

Only seven Newcastles met in Neuburg (New Castle, Pennsylvania having been unable to attend,) but there were 53 visiting delegates plus the hosts, many more than the 30 who had attended in 2006 and matching the number who had visited the USA in 2002. Newcastle upon Tyne sent an official municipal delegation for the first time, having previously been represented privately. The summit theme was business (especially 'green' business) and economic development.

2010 Newcastle, South Africa

With the greater distances involved (and perhaps because they had hosted previously) the number of delegates to Newcastle South Africa in 2010 was fewer than in 2008.

Of the original founders Newcastle-under-Lyme and New Castle, Pennsylvania were missing in addition to Neufchâteau who attended only the first conference. The main conference theme was supporting young people and their aspirations.

The conference in South Africa took the decision to ask Newcastle upon Tyne not only to host the next summit but to act as a secretariat between conferences to improve communications and continuity.

2012 Newcastle upon Tyne, UK

The 2012 summit saw representatives from Kota Bharu (Malaysia), Akhaltsikhe (Georgia), Newcastle in New South Wales (Australia), Jaunpils (Latvia), Newcastle in Ontario (Canada) and Nové Hrady (Czech Republic) present for the first time, alongside Neuburg, Shinshiro, Neuchâtel, Newcastle South Africa, Newcastle-under-Lyme and the hosts, a total of eighty-three visiting delegates discussing the topic of how the Newcastles promote themselves and win more tourists.

2014 Nové Hrady, Czech Republic

Nové Hrady kindly agreed to host the 2014 conference, being the smallest of the host Newcastles to date. The theme was how we make best use of our culture, heritage, buildings and ecology to promote our Newcastles, and over sixty delegates from ten different Newcastles participated, including Nyborg (Denmark) for the first time.

2016 Newcastle, Canada

By the time we met in Newcastle in Canada in 2016 we had also been joined by Nové Zámky in Slovakia and we were pleased to welcome back representatives from both New Castles, Indiana and Pennsylvania. This made a record total of thirteen different Newcastle being represented at the conference where our main theme was 'age-friendly Newcastles, responding to the challenges and opportunities of an ageing population'

2018 Shinshiro, Japan

Our conferences create a platform for both taking stock of progress and identifying areas for cooperation up to the subsequent conference. We enjoy the hospitality of the host Newcastles and finding out about their towns, each with their distinctive cultural and heritage. In recent years it has also been possible to ensure that sufficient young people are amongst our delegations for them to have their own discussions and present proposals for working together and ensuring that their voice is heard. So much so that our very first dedicated youth conference was held in Shinshiro in December 2017 with ten Newcastles sending thirty youth delegates, and a similar number from the host city who so generously proposed and supported the initiative. In 2018, we return to where it all started for the 20th anniversary conference at Shinshiro.

Newcastles of the World Youth Conference, Shinshiro, Japan, 2017.

The Projects

In the early days of the alliance most collaborative working was directly between individual Newcastles - for example equipment provided by Neuburg an der Donau, Germany for township schools in Newcastle South Africa.

With Newcastle upon Tyne acting as a permanent secretariat, albeit initially only with volunteer input, there was more opportunity for project work among different Newcastles between conferences. During 2011 plans were evolved for several projects.

'Proud to Call it Home' is a poetry anthology compiled from poems written by people in several Newcastles - from Australia, Canada, Germany, Japan, South Africa, Switzerland and the UK. Contributors wrote about their own Newcastle, with newly-commissioned work by Wajid Hussain, Catherine Graham and Sheree Mack from Newcastle upon Tyne, and a foreword (and poem) from Lindiwe Mabuza. She is a internationally-acclaimed South African politician, diplomat (former High Commisisoner), writer and academic who was born in 1938 in Newcastle, KwaZulu Natal. The poetry anthology was published on-line and in printed format.

'This is my Home Newcastle' was a music project which involved several Newcastles creating their own lyrics to a common musical score. This is based on 'Home Newcastle', a song which was a minor 'hit' record in Newcastle upon Tyne. Each participating Newcastle recorded their own version performed by several different types of singers and musicians - a male voice choir, individual singers, school choirs, barbers' shop quartet, as well as instrumental versions – all to the common tune.

Newcastle upon Tyne used its hosting of the 2012 conference to showcase a number of these projects as well as a project to create a commemorative 'proggy mat' (a local craft for the making of rugs - in this case intended for display - out of sections of unwanted cloth cut into strips and pulled through a hessian backing). This was designed and overseen by local craftswomen but many delegates who attended the 2012 conference contributed personally by 'progging' a section of the rug.

A major exhibition of stamps, franked letters and other philatelic material collected from and about Newcastles around the world was displayed in Newcastle upon Tyne main library (and other libraries) also in 2012; the collection had been built by the late Dorothy Martin over almost thirty years.

Once some members of the alliance began making annual financial contributions towards the running of the network it became possible for part-time project staff to be engaged to support the project work of the volunteers. For example, this allowed the development of the 'Global Schools' project which formalised some pre-existing bilateral links between individual schools in different Newcastles through professionally-prepared material for participating schools. This took the form of an introductory pack with curriculum resources and ideas for making friendship links with their partner school, which the secretariat helped broker.

Alongside a growing number of youth exchanges - given additional momentum through our first-ever dedicated youth conference in Shinshiro in late 2017 - the most important of our projects is the 'Newcastles Passport'. This scheme promotes tourism and friendship between Newcastles around the world. Each Newcastle taking part has carefully selected a series of special offers just for visitors from other Newcastles. These could be a customised programme if the visitor has any special interests – places to visit or people to meet, or special discounts from local businesses. Visitors sign up for a free 'Passport' through our website, then get in touch with the Newcastle they wish to visit. Each Newcastle is committed to offering a personalised touch, with a warm and friendly welcome to anyone living in an affiliated Newcastle. To date Newcastles in Japan, Switzerland, Germany, the United Kingdom, Georgia and the USA (New Castle, Pennsylvania) are formally part of this exciting initiative.

Following the 2014 conference in Nové Hrady the 'Newcastles Forum' was set up as an online platform for the exchange of ideas and opinions on topics of shared interest, to complement that section of the alliance website where papers of common interest are posted.

Business links have proved harder to develop but opportunities have been taken to invite one Newcastle to attend trade exhibitions hosted in another. A delegation of municipal and business people from Newcastle KwaZulu Natal visited Newcastle upon Tyne in 2015 for an international trade event between the UK and South Africa designed to coincide with the Rugby World Cup; this led to a subsequent delegation from the North East Chamber of Commerce visiting the South African Newcastle during a return visit and signing a memorandum of understanding with the Chamber of Commerce branch there.

Cultural projects and exchanges are perhaps understandably easier to create and develop. In 2017, Nové Hrady organised a project which they called 'Spring in Newcastles' - an exhibition of photos and paintings provided by several different Newcastles of spring scenes in their own towns and cities. This exhibition is also planned to be shown in other Newcastles including Nové Zamky, Slovakia. Young singers, musicians and dancers from Newcastle, South Africa and Newcastle upon Tyne performed with hosts in Akhaltsikhe in the summer of 2017 at the Georgian city's annual cultural festival. The 'Two Newcastles' project linking artists from Newcastle upon Tyne and Newcastle South Africa has been underway since 2016, sharing through drama and music the experiences of young people in those two very different environments. And there is a 'Newcastles of the World' songbook.

Shinshiro and Neuchâtel have developed a very fruitful co-operation which has led to Neuchâtel City Council enabling young people from their city to travel to Shinshiro to take up a one-year work placement in the municipality. The initiative got underway with the International Team in Shinshiro hosting a very successful placement and deciding to welcome other young people from Neuchâtel on placement and relocate a member of Shinshiro's International Team to Neuchâtel. The links are going from strength to strength, providing opportunities to experience each other's cultures, languages and life at work.

At the time of production of this book other projects are under way or being considered including a Newcastles of the World cook book, and a potential collaboration between Newcastles within Europe around tourism as well as new projects with a greater focus on connecting young people as Newcastles of the World looks forward to the next twenty years and beyond.

Proud To Call It Home

Newcastles of the World

Colorow Trail,
Newcastle,
Colorado.

The Future

In the years ahead we hope that more of the 'Newcastles' of which we are aware will choose to participate in our projects and will be willing to exchange their knowledge and experience of the issues that affect us all. This may simply be via electronic means, or by attending our biennial conferences, but we expect that it will also include two or more Newcastles, perhaps of similar size, collaborating on matters of common interest. Not all will choose to engage in every project.

Nor will the alliance remain largely dependent – as it still is at present – upon the support and leadership of the municipalities that bear our name. Local government in many parts of the world faces severe financial pressures and sadly finds it less easy to commit the time or resource to international projects. Others, at times of financial retrenchment, nevertheless see this as even more important than before - investing time and effort in international networking to raise their profiles, gain new friends, influence decision-makers and learn new ideas and practices through cooperation. There is potential strength in collective lobbying and through coordinated access to funding, fresh ideas, and influential people and agencies.

However, this is a route not only to economic benefit or additional tourism but to success through sharing learning and best practice. This is because we believe that there is much scope for collaborations that promote language, learning, culture and a wider understanding of the world for their own sakes. We are therefore encouraged by the growing interest of our young people in coming together and learning from their counterparts in other Newcastles, and making new friendships which we are sure will last a lifetime.

So whilst mayors and other political leaders may change, as may their interests and priorities, we expect the future success of Newcastles of the World to be about how we also increasingly engage and help connect voluntary and community agencies, chambers of commerce, our youth councils and educational institutions and other local organisations whose work so enriches our communities.

That said, we are truly indebted to the continued participation, enthusiasm and commitment of those Newcastles whose political leaderships have been at the core of our work from the outset, in particular Shinshiro City, Neuchâtel and Neuburg an der Donau. The recent growth in the number of Newcastles who are actively involved in our work has been made possible because these core members have 'stayed the course' and been an inspiration to us all.

Appendix I

www.newcastlesoftheworld.com
www.facebook.com/nclsoftheworld/ @NCLsftheworld
Room 243, Civic Centre, Newcastle upon Tyne, United Kingdom NE1 8QH
Tel +44 (0) 191 211 6828 Mobile +44 (0)7717 223600
newcastlesoftheworld@gmail.com

CHARTER OF NEWCASTLES OF THE WORLD

Newcastles of the World is a friendship alliance that brings together in a single network towns and cities that share the name 'Newcastle' in their own language. It was established in 1998 by the Mayor of Shinshiro City in Japan. The core members of the alliance meet every two years.

Aims

To build friendship between people and organisations in different Newcastles, to further understanding of different countries and cultures through its activities, to develop projects of mutual benefit and to share best practice in areas of common interest so that we can learn from each other.

Governance

The biennial conference reviews progress and sets the targets for the next two years ahead; these are developed through discussion and approved by a session at the end of each conference by the mayors and mayoral representatives. This is set out in a conference report/declaration which is then presented to the full conference before it ends and posted on our website.

The next conference will be in Shinshiro City, Japan in October 2018. The hosts in 2020 will be the city of Neuchâtel in Switzerland.

Between conferences, every other year a Leaders' board of all mayors or mayoral representatives of those Newcastles who contribute towards the running costs of the alliance will communicate, either by meeting together or by tele-conference or similar, to review progress and decide on any changes or new initiatives.

Between these annual discussions, a Leaders' executive Board of nominated Newcastles will communicate approximately every six months or at any other time that urgent business might need to be discussed, either by meeting together or by tele-conference or similar, to review progress and decide on any changes or new initiatives. Between the 2016 and 2018 conferences the Leaders' Executive Board members will comprise Neuchâtel, Neuburg, Nyborg, Nové Hrady and Shinshiro City. At the 2018 conference, Leaders' Executive Board members for the period to 2020 will be chosen.

The Leaders' Board and Leaders' Executive Board will be supported by a Secretariat whose running costs will be paid for by contributions from those Newcastles who are able and willing to make payment. The biennial conference will decide where the

Secretariat will be based. Currently it is based in Newcastle upon Tyne, United Kingdom. Funds from contributing Newcastles will be used to pay for the time of one or more project managers to promote and support the work programme of the alliance, as agreed at conference. This work will be overseen by someone in the community where the Secretariat is located, on a voluntary, unpaid basis, on behalf of the mayors. Currently this is David Faulkner.

The Secretariat

The Secretariat will report twice a year to the Leaders' Board on progress and on the finances of the alliance. This report will form the basis of the subsequent discussions of the Leaders' Board and Leaders' Executive Board, plus any other issues that members wish to raise for consideration.

The core tasks of the Secretariat are to maintain and develop a database of contacts in Newcastles across the world and to connect them by quarterly newsletters, social media and day-to-day communication as appropriate; to support and help deliver the agreed work programme and projects of the alliance, to facilitate the sharing of best practice information, to help arrange visits between Newcastles; to manage the day-to-day business and finances of the alliance; to promote and publicise Newcastles of the World to existing and new audiences; to research and contact additional Newcastles around the world; to produce a range of material for information centres and exhibitions.

Contributions by Members

Newcastles who subscribe are contributing to the running costs of our alliance, are able to take part in decisions about the future priorities, major projects and policies of the alliance, and receive best attention from the Secretariat.

There is no set membership 'fee' as such - members pay what they can afford according to their size and resources, but the minimum expectation is 1,000 euros or equivalent per annum. Larger Newcastles pay more but that is their choice, and we are grateful for their commitment. Newcastles who do not wish to pay a subscription fee may still receive newsletters and other communications, can share in some activities (such as school links and sharing of best practice information) and may attend as guests at the biennial conferences at their cost.

Appendix II

PLEASE COMPLETE THIS FORM IN CAPITAL LETTERS

Name of your village, town or city ....
Location (province and country) ....
Population ....
Website address ....

Names and email addresses:
Mayor or other political leader..
Chief Executive Officer or other most senior official.......................................
Main official for tourism...
Main official for education ....
Main official for business/economic development ....
Main official for culture/heritage ....
Your media or public relations officer ....

Do you have a youth council or similar organisation where young people in your
Newcastle come together to express views and organise events? YES/NO
If yes,please give a contact name and email address:
....

Do you have an elders' council or similar where older people in your Newcastle come
together to express their views and organise events and services? YES/NO
If yes, please give a contact name and email address if you can
....

Name and email address of the person who would be your main contact for
Newcastles of the World
....
....

Spoken and written languages of this person
....

Would someone from your Newcastle wish to attend our next Newcastles of the World
conference in Shinshiro, Japan, October 2018?
PROBABLY YES/PROBABLY NO/WE WILL CONSIDER THIS

Would you like us to link one or more of your local schools with one in another
Newcastle ?
YES - NOW / YES - LATER / NO
If yes now, please give (or attach) name of school and contact details there
....

Please tell us what you most hope to achieve and/or contribute by being part of the
Newcastles alliance?

WE APPLY TO BECOME A MEMBER OF NEWCASTLES OF THE WORLD

Name

....

Title

....

Signature

....

Date

....

Do you wish to become a subscribing (paying) member of the Newcastles of the World alliance ?

YES - please invoice us for the amount of .... Euros / NO / WE WILL CONSIDER THIS

Newcastles who subscribe are contributing to the running costs of our alliance, are able to take part in decisions about the future priorities, major projects and policies of the alliance, and receive best attention from our team. There is no set membership 'fee' as such - members pay what they can afford according to their size and resources, but the minimum expectation is 1,000 euros or equivalent per annum. Larger Newcastles pay more but that is their choice, and we are grateful for their commitment.

Newcastles who do not wish to pay a subscription fee still receive newsletters and other communications, can share in some activities (such as school links and sharing of best practice information) and may attend as paying guests at our conferences which take place every two years - 2018 in Japan, 2020 in Switzerland.

Please return this form to David Faulkner - david.faulkner@newcastle.gov.uk, tel 0044 (0)7717 223600, or contact him for further information or if you have any queries.

newcastlesoftheworld.com
facebook.com/nclsoftheworld
twitter.com/NCLSoftheworld
newcastlesforum.com

Tyne
Bridge
Publishing